YOUR WORDS

YOUR WORDS

LEARNING THE LANGUAGE OF THE KINGDOM

Wendy Starr
Amos 5:14

WENDY COOPER STARR

Pleasant Word
A Division of WinePress Group
PW

Pleasant Word (a division of WinePress Publishing, PO Box 428, Enumclaw, WA 98022) functions only as book publisher. As such, the ultimate design, content, editorial accuracy, and views expressed or implied in this work are those of the author.

ISBN 13: 978-1-4141-1631-0
ISBN 10: 1-4141-1631-4
Library of Congress Catalog Card Number: 2009911103

Set a watch, O Lord, before my mouth;
keep the door of my lips.
Psalm 141:3 (KJV)

May the words of my mouth
and the meditation of my heart
be acceptable in your sight,
O LORD, my Strength and my Redeemer.
Psalm 19:14 (NKJV)

If ye continue in my word,
then are ye my disciples indeed;
and you shall know the truth,
and the truth shall make you free.
John 8:31, 32 (KJV)

Whoso offereth praise glorifieth me:
and to him that ordereth his conversation aright
will I show the salvation of God.
Psalm 50:23 (KJV)

Seek good, and not evil, that ye may live:
and so the LORD, the God of hosts,
shall be with you, as ye have spoken.
Amos 5:14 (KJV)

CONTENTS

INTRODUCTION

I FIRST STUDIED and taught on the importance of words in a small women's Bible study. We called it the Upper Room Bible Study because it met every Thursday evening at my law office which was at that time on the second floor of our building. The Bible study on the importance of words changed our thoughts, our hearts, and our lives. The women from that first study have gone on to teach their families and friends about the importance of words. We have seen exciting results as others get a revelation of the importance of how they use words.

I must admit that when I first heard a sermon on words, I became defensive and dismissive. My first response was that I was hearing new age philosophy cloaked in evangelical rhetoric. But the speaker told us we were not to take his word for what he was sharing with us. He told us to get in the Bible, find out what God had to say about the importance of our words, and then change our beliefs and actions to conform to God's Word.

The Upper Room Bible Study on words and this book are the result of my personal search to find out what God had to say about words and specifically about the impact my words have on my life. I have only one life to live on this earth. It is so brief. It is so easily squandered. I believe what I say, in faith believing, creates my life. I believe what you speak from your heart creates all the good and all the bad in your life. I believe when you do not thoughtfully use words, life will knock you around. Instead of taking dominion over the circumstances in your life, you will be at the mercy of the world's system.

God used words to create. Read the first chapter of Genesis. Before the beginning, God existed. Then, in the beginning, God created the heaven and earth. But the earth was empty and dark. Then God spoke. He saw darkness but He spoke light. Nine times in the seven days of creation God spoke first and then it was so. God called things that were not as though they were, and what He spoke became real in the natural world. Creation did not happen because God wanted it and expected it and planned for it. Creation happened because God spoke.

Words are thoughts being spoken. God never did anything without saying it first. The plan of salvation was spoken time and again by various men over hundreds of years throughout the Old Testament before it happened.

As a human being, you were created above every other aspect of creation. You were created in the image and likeness of God. And you were created to exercise dominion over the natural world. What you say is important because you say what you really believe (Psalm 116:10, Matthew 15:18) and because you get what you say (because you believe it). At a minimum, your words reflect your relationship and obedience to Christ; at a deeper level, you prophesy your future by the words you speak.

Do not use your personal life experiences to dismiss this fact. Study God's Word and see what He has to say about it and then decide what you are going to do about it.

Don't dismiss this book as espousing a "blab it and grab it" philosophy or as another teaching that implies humans can manipulate God. Don't think this book places material wealth above everything. The only request I have of you is that you determine to read these words with a mind that is open to the leading of the Holy Spirit. Do not dismiss what is written here before you read it. Do not believe what you read here because you think it sounds good. Go to God's Word. Check out what is written there. Once you see what God has to say, believe and act on that.

THE KINGDOM OF GOD

But seek ye first the kingdom of God, and His righteousness; and all these things shall be added unto you.

—Matthew 6:33 (KJV) See also Luke 12:31

The kingdom of God cometh not with observation. Neither shall they say, Lo here! or, lo there! for behold, the kingdom of God is within you.

—Luke 17:20-21 (KJV)

For the kingdom of God is not meat and drink; but righteousness, and peace, and joy in the Holy Ghost.

—Romans 14:17 (KJV)

For the kingdom of God is not in word but in power.

—1 Corinthians 4:20 (KJV)

THE SUBTITLE OF this book is *Learning the Language of the Kingdom*. Why? How is what you and I say related to the kingdom of God?

When Jesus was on the earth, He went about preaching the gospel of the kingdom; the good news of the kingdom. And I believe Jesus' death and resurrection ushered in the Kingdom of God on the earth.

The Oxford English Dictionary defines kingdom as, "an organized community headed by a king; the territory subject to a king; the spiritual reign attributed to God; the sphere of this kingdom…"[1] Is the entire world an organized community headed by God as king? No. Is the body of Christ, the Church, an organized community headed by King Jesus? Yes. Ephesians 2:19 tells us we are citizens of the household of God. We know we are in the world but that we are not of the world.

As new creations in Christ Jesus, we should be living under God's authority. We should, right now, be living by the laws and principles that govern God's kingdom. We will live by them for eternity. We should be learning them and living by them now. I submit to you that when you and I get serious about living according to God's laws now, we will live in victory, in peace and joy in the Holy Ghost, and in power.

Besides geography, in the world's system, kingdoms or countries are identified by, among other things, their language, currency, customs, and laws. Learning what God says about our speech is learning the language of His kingdom.

Before we learn what God says about our speech, let's take a minute to look at the two kingdoms that are currently operational in the earth: the kingdom of God (Luke 17:21) and the kingdom of Satan (Luke 11:18). Each kingdom has certain characteristics that identify it.

The kingdom of God exists within humans who speak the word of God in faith; in humans who are in a covenant relationship with the God of creation. The kingdom of

Satan exists in humans who use words filled with doubt and unbelief.

Angels operate within the kingdom of God. Angels worship God (Hebrews 1:6; Revelation 7:11). They minister for us; not to us (Hebrews 1:14). They protect us (Psalm 91:11). We will judge them (1 Corinthians 6:3). They hear and obey the voice of God's word (Psalms 103:20). Demons operate within the kingdom of Satan. Demons hate humans and only obey humans if they worship Satan or if they are speaking God's word. Every knee must bow to the authority of Jesus (Philippians 2:10). Demons always obeyed Jesus and they must always obey you when you speak to them in Jesus' name (His authority).

The kingdom of God is powered by love. The kingdom of Satan is powered by fear.

The kingdom of God is governed by the law of grace through faith. The kingdom of Satan is governed by the law of sin and death. Christians need to get a revelation of this fact: we are new creatures who are not bound by the law of sin and death. Period. You may say, "But I try and try and I can't get victory." I submit that you are trying in your own strength instead of resting in the finished work of Christ. In the United States, all slaves were freed by the federal government in 1865. But it took 100 more years for African Americans to choose to walk in that freedom. Brother and sister, you are a new creation in Christ Jesus. It is time you choose to walk in the freedom and victory Jesus gives. Now. You need to study the law of grace and make a decision to receive it, apply it, and watch it change your life.

The kingdom of God is not comprised of material things but rather of righteousness, peace, and joy in the Holy Spirit (Romans 14:17). The kingdom of Satan is comprised of what we see, hear, touch, and smell; of temporal things. One definition of temporal is "enduring for a short time;

transitory; short-lived."[2] Temporal things are subject to change. One of the most powerful change agents of temporal things is, as you shall see, your spoken words.

The kingdom of God is evidenced not by words but in power (1 Corinthians 4:20). The kingdom of Satan is evidenced by perversion. Consider the black mass, a perversion of our remembrance of the covenant to which we are beneficiaries. Consider Satan's perversion of sex and music. Consider Satan's perversion of the home. Fear is a perversion of faith. Deception is a perversion of truth. Satan cannot create so he perverts what God creates.

The motto of the economy of the kingdom of God is "live to give" (Proverbs 11:24-25; Luke 6:38). Jesus was such a giver that when Judas left during the last supper, the other disciples thought he was going to give to the poor. Christians who walk in their kingdom authority understand that God is their provider. They do not look to their employer, their family, or their government for what they need. They understand they are blessed to be a blessing to others. The motto of the economy of the kingdom of Satan could be "live to get."

Although the kingdom of God and the kingdom of Satan are opposites in most respects, both work essentially the same way: presentment, acceptance, manifestation. Humans are generally presented with a thought. It can be a righteous thought, an evil thought, or a neutral thought. The only decision we must make is whether to accept the thought and act on it or to reject it.

James 1:13-15 discuss how we end up in sin. When we are presented with a sinful thought and we allow it to remain, we dwell on it, we meditate on it, and it is then conceived in our heart. We will speak and act on it, and the sin will then manifest. That end is death.

In the alternative, when we are presented with potentially sinful thoughts, which are really simply opportunities to sin, we can cast down that imagination along with every other high thing that exalts itself against the knowledge of God and bring into captivity every thought to the obedience of Christ (2 Corinthians 10:5). That end is righteousness, peace, and joy in the Holy Ghost. That end is living in the power and victory that Jesus died to give you.

The battle for humanity is real. It is a battle between God and Satan. It has not been an eternal battle, but the outcome will be eternal. Everyone living by the laws of the kingdom of God must continually fight the kingdom of Satan, and we do that by willingly and confidently engaging in the spiritual battle wherever it manifests. Ephesians 6 and Romans 13:12 tell us how to recognize the enemy (it's not flesh and blood) and how to engage the enemy (by putting on the armor of light).

I submit to you that the easiest way to defeat Satan is to make a quality decision to stay out of strife in all situations. When you allow strife, you are inviting into your life confusion and every evil work (James 3:16). I believe choosing forgiveness over strife is advanced Christianity. New Christians and Christians who have not grown into the meat of the Word are not very successful with this choice. Strife is a mindset of the kingdom of Satan. Forgiveness is the mindset of Christ and of His kingdom. It is time Christians understand that persecution will come because it arises for the word's sake. We should be quick to redirect our anger away from other people and toward the instigator of all persecution and strife: Satan.

Once you have made a quality decision to stay out of strife in all situations: with your spouse, your children, your employer, your pastor, your neighbor, stand on that decision. Do not allow yourself to be moved from it. As with most things in life, staying out of strife does not just happen. It becomes easier with practice. You must choose to enforce your decision every day; multiple times each day.

In addition to refusing to be in strife (which includes refusing to be offended), you need to be constantly vigilant (1 Peter 5:8) so that you give no place to the devil (Ephesians 4:27; Job 3:25). You need to constantly check your covering (Romans 13:12, Matthew 6:22, and Ephesians 6). You must submit to God and actively resist the devil (James 4:7). You must speak the word of God into every situation and after having done all this, you simply stand (Ephesians 6:13) and watch what God will do on your behalf.

Our ways of doing things for God in the natural have worn us out. We try to please God. We try to find God's face. We should be concerned that we are wasting time with no fruit because we insist on using our own fleshly (natural) efforts instead of operating in His system, according to the laws and customs of His kingdom.

I believe it is time we learn the language of the kingdom. I believe we will use it for eternity.

STUDY GUIDE

1. A kingdom is an ______________________________
2. According to Luke 17:21(KJV), where is the kingdom of God? ______________________________
3. According to Philippians 3:20 (NIV), where is our citizenship? ______________________________
4. Besides geographic location, list three things that distinguish countries?

   a.

   b.

   c.
5. What two kingdoms are operational in the spirit realms?

   a.

   b.
6. List the distinctions between the kingdom of God and the kingdom of Satan.

   a.

   b.

   c.

   d.

   e.

   f.

   g.
7. What changes do you need to make in your thinking in order to live according to God's system of doing things?

YOU ARE A NEW CREATION, NOW TALK LIKE ONE

And God said, Let us make man in our image, after our likeness: and let them have dominion over the fish of the sea, and over the fowl of the air, and over the cattle, and over all the earth, and over every creeping thing that creeps upon the earth. So God created man in his own image, in the image of God created he him; male and female created he them.

—Genesis 1:26–27 (KJV)

If any man be in Christ, he is a new creature: old things are passed away; behold, all things are become new.

—2 Corinthians 5:17 (KJV)

YOU ARE HUMAN. That means you were created in the image and likeness of God; God intended it to be so. Through the first Adam, sin entered the world and man became less than he was created to be. Then the second Adam, Jesus, came and it became possible for man to choose to be restored to the image and likeness of God.

If you have chosen Christ, if you are in Christ, you are a new creature. Did Paul intend this to be a figurative expression or were you actually transformed into a new kind of creature? Satan would have you believe the lie that you are not re-created until your physical death. But we are spirit beings; our essence is spirit. We have souls (mind, will, and emotions) and we live in a body, but we are spirits. Our bodies allow us to visit earth, and our bodies are most likely why we can be easily deceived into believing Paul was being figurative.

Revelation 1:6 says Jesus "has made us kings and priests unto God and his Father." Notice, Jesus *has* made us, not *will* make us. Being kings and priests now may give us new responsibilities and new authority, but it does not make us new creatures.

Paul was not using the term "new creature" (some translations say "new creation") figuratively. He tells us we are a new kind of being. I believe everyone who is "in Christ" is no longer a fallen, helpless, and powerless being destined to live in darkness. I believe everyone who is in Christ is a royal, powerful being of light destined to live in The Light.

This isn't some kind of futuristic fantasy. This is real. We are a new kind of creature; one that could not exist until Jesus lived and died and rose again. We are spirit beings who have been lifted from the filth of the world, washed by the blood of Jesus and the water of the Word, and re-created in the image and likeness of God. But what exactly does that mean? And why in the narrative of the creation of humans did God use two words, *image* and *likeness*?

The Hebrew word that is translated *image* in Genesis 1:26 is *tselem* and it means to shade; a phantom; illusion; figure; resemblance.[3] I think of an image as the thing seen in a photograph or a hologram. An image is derived from the very person or object portrayed. That person or thing must be present for the image to be made. It is not the object or person, it is not a replica of the object or person, but an image is part of the essence – part of what makes the person or thing unique.

The Hebrew word that is translated *likeness* in Genesis 1:26 is *demuth* and it means resemblance, model, shape, like.[4] A likeness has the same general shape as the original such as a toy car or a wooden giraffe. A caricature is also a likeness. The original is not always present when a likeness is made, but a likeness is enough like the original that you recognize the original in the likeness.

And so it is with us. In some ways, we are like God yet different from Him. We are God's likeness when we are loving. God is love (1 John 4:8). We are not love itself but we can love. God is life but we have life; we live (Genesis 2:7). God is the Prince of Peace (Isaiah 9:6); we have God's peace (John 14:27). God is light; we live in the light (1 John 1:5-7). God is true; we tell the truth (John 3:33-35). When we live this way, others can recognize God in us. People who do not know God personally can also demonstrate God's likeness. He created humanity to have His attributes. We were all created in His likeness.

In other ways we are, or can be, exactly like God; we are His image. Although that does not in any way make us equal with God, it does make us exactly like Him in some key areas. For example, God is a spirit; I am a spirit. I have a soul and I live in a body, but I am a spirit. God is holy; I am to be holy (set apart) (1 Peter 1:15, 16). God lives by faith; I am to live by faith (Habakkuk 2:4, Romans 1:17, Galatians 3:11, Hebrews 10:38). God is merciful (Psalm 116:5) and I am to be merciful (Luke 6:36). God forgives (1 John 1:9) and I am to forgive (Matthew 18:21, 22; Luke 17:4). God is no respecter of persons (Acts 10:34) and I am not to be a respecter of people (James 2). God speaks things that are not into existence (Romans 4:17) and as we shall see, we speak things into existence. God is king of all the earth (Psalm 47:7) and, in the authority restored to man by Jesus, I am to have dominion over all the earth (Genesis 1:26, Psalm 8:6).

Each of us must choose whether to exhibit God likeness (godliness) and to live by kingdom principles or to allow fleshly lusts to prevail and to be subject to the world system. Each of us, because we are essentially spirit beings, is bound by spiritual laws. We can choose to use those spiritual laws to bring good things into our lives as God intended, or we can live our lives with spiritual laws perverted to work havoc in our lives. Again, the choice is ours.

Even as Satan lied to Adam and Eve in the Garden when he convinced them to doubt God's Word, he lies to us today. Tradition tells us the original sin was disobedience: eating the fruit of the forbidden tree. Adam and Eve did disobey God; however, I believe their original sin was choosing to believe what the serpent said rather than choosing to believe God. Our choice today is the same choice as the one presented in the Garden. Who will you believe?

I invite you to choose to believe God. Jesus came to give us life and that life more abundantly (John 10:10). You are created in the image and the likeness of God. When you became a new creation in Christ Jesus, you were restored to a position of authority and dominion. Jesus gave that possibility to you, but the choice to live in that position is yours. God longs to breathe His Spirit into you every day so that day by day, as you yield to the Spirit, you manifest Him. Paul taught the outward signs of religion are irrelevant; that being a new creation is all that matters (Galatians 6:15).

You were created with the authority for dominion (to tread down; prevail against; rule) over nature (Genesis 1:26) and now, in Christ, over all things (Psalm 8:6; John 14:12-14).

The Holy Spirit provides *dunamius* or the physical, explosive power and Jesus' Name gives you *exucia* or authority, but you must choose to walk in them.

Even as God is a tri-part being, we are tri-part beings. The battle between light and darkness and, ultimately, the battle for humanity takes place in the human mind. The mind, the will, and the emotions make up the soul of man. When my mind, will, and emotions (soul) line up with what my body wants to do, I live in the world's system and I am in evil territory. Conversely, when my mind lines up with what my regenerated spirit wants to do, I dwell in the secret place of the Most High and I stay under the shadow of the Almighty (Psalm 91). When my spirit and soul are operating in unity, God will give me whatever I ask (Matthew 18:19).

Jesus prayed for you, and He gave you His glory (John 17:20-23). Why? So you and I could be one with Jesus and the Father. Are you one with Jesus? If you are, you will talk like Jesus and act like Jesus. You will believe that with God all things are possible (Matthew 19:26, Mark 9:23, Mark 10:27). You will live a life of victory even as you deal with the problems that impact you because you live on the planet earth; the fallen, wicked, beautiful, alluring place where you presently live.

Believe one of the ways you are to be exactly like God is to use your words as vehicles to carry your faith. Jesus did. The alternative is that you use your words to carry your doubt, your unbelief, and your fear. You are a spirit being and this is a spiritual law: one way or the other, words create. The choice is yours.

He that orders his conversation (which includes behavior) aright shall see the salvation (liberty, deliverance, prosperity) of God (Psalm 50:23).

STUDY GUIDE

1. And God said, Let us make man in our __________, after our __________: and let them have __________ over the fish of the sea, and over the fowl of the air, and over the cattle, and over all the earth, and over every creeping thing that creeps upon the earth. So God created man in his __________, in the image of God created he him; male and female created he them (Genesis 1:26–27 KJV).
2. If __________ man be in Christ, he __________ a __________: old things are passed away: behold, all things are become new (2 Corinthians 5:17 KJV).
3. Revelation 1:6 (KJV) says Jesus "__________ made us __________ unto God and his Father."
4. In Christ, I am a __________, __________ being of __________.
5. "*Image*" means __________.

   "*Likeness*"means __________.
6. How are we "like" God? __________

   ____
7. How are we an exact image of God? __________

   ____
8. Galatians 6:15 (KJV) says the outward signs of religion are irrelevant; all that matters is being a __________.
9. You were created with the power for dominion (to __________, __________, __________) over nature (Genesis 1:26) and now, in Christ, over __________ things (Psalm 8:6; John 14:12-13).

10. The Holy Spirit gives us __________ or the physical, explosive power and Jesus' name gives us __________, the authority, but we must __________ to walk in them.

11. My words either carry my ________ or my ________, __________ and __________. The choice is ________.

12. List three verses that describe ways Christians manifest God's image and likeness.

    a.

    b.

    c.

13. Do you feel like a new creature/creation (2 Corinthians 5:17)? Why or why not?

14. What does Galatians 6:15 mean to you?

15. What does it mean to you to have Jesus' glory and to be one with Jesus and the Father (John 17:20-23)?

16. What are some changes you need to make to walk in Jesus' glory and to be one with Jesus and the Father?

WITH THE MOUTH CONFESSION IS MADE UNTO SALVATION

But what does it say? "The word is near you, in your mouth and in your heart" (that is, the word of faith which we preach):that if you confess with your mouth the Lord Jesus and believe in your heart that God has raised Him from the dead, you will be saved. For with the heart one believes unto righteousness, and with the mouth confession is made unto salvation.

—Romans 10:8-10 (NKJ)

WE USUALLY THINK the word *salvation* means to be saved from hell. I have often said that the church has been quite good at scaring the hell out of people. Many people go forward in church services to "accept Jesus as their Savior" because they do not want to go to hell but not because they want to follow Jesus. They have no intention of allowing Jesus to be Lord of their lives. They are not told Jesus wants them to choose Him. We get people saved, but because we often do not mentor them or help them grow into a deep relationship with Jesus, many are left to live a life void of victory.

The Greek word translated in Romans 10: 8-10 as *saved* is *sozo*. It is a verb that means to deliver, protect, preserve, heal, and make whole.[5] The word translated *salvation* is *soteria,* and it is the noun that means rescue, deliverance, protection, preservation, health, wholeness, salvation.[6]

What Paul is telling us in Romans is that when we open our mouths and say with understanding and belief that Jesus is our Lord (master, ruler, superior); when we confess that Jesus has the right to tell us what to do, when to do it, and how to do it; and when we simultaneously believe in our hearts that God has raised Jesus from the dead; we are delivered, protected, preserved, healed, and made whole. How great is that!

My question to all you who know you are going to heaven when you die is, do you also know you are delivered now, protected now, preserved now, healed now, and made whole now? You won't need to be delivered or protected in heaven. Salvation is for your life now, here on earth. But it is not automatic. You can be headed for heaven but still live on earth as someone has said, "sick, busted, and disgusted."

Paul tells us while it is with the heart that we believe unto righteousness, it is with our mouth that we claim our deliverance, our protection, our preservation, our healing and our wholeness. Paul says it is not enough to just believe. We must open our mouths and confess our soteria. The solution to every problem we face is in the Word of God that we speak with our mouth.

We must choose to confess God's word over our circumstances even when we do not see any end in sight; even when we are so sick we can't stand up; even when we are so broke we don't even have any pennies in our pocket; even when our loved ones hang up every time we phone them; even when we lose our job. We must open our mouth and with joy and confidence declare the word of God.

Speak it to ourselves when no one else is listening. Speak it to ourselves when everyone else is listening; even when they mock us. In whatever situation we find ourselves, in agony and despair, in disappointment and loss, in joy and prosperity, in health and in happiness, speak God's word into that situation.

When all seems lost, keep speaking His word for His words are spirit and they are life (John 6:63). Joel 3:10 says let the weak say, "I am strong." It does not say let the weak pray, "Let me become strong." Are we to pray? Absolutely yes, we are to pray without ceasing. But God will not do for us what He has told us to do for ourselves. The weak should pray that God will reveal to them what to do to become strong even as they say out loud, "I am strong."

Matthew tells us about a Roman soldier, a centurion, who understood that words carry authority. He asked Jesus to "speak the word only" to heal his servant. Jesus said the man had great faith. This man clearly understood that authority needed to be spoken to be effective. And He understood that Jesus had only to speak words of healing and healing had to come (Matthew 8:5-10). Because of the cross and the resurrection, we have Jesus' authority—and Jesus has authority over everything. But in order to release His authority in our lives, we must open our mouths and speak faith-filled words.

We don't just recite words we wish would work. We don't speak from our fear of the circumstances or from our doubt that God will really meet our need this time, in time. We speak from our knowledge of who God is. We speak from our knowledge of His Word. We speak His words into our situation. The words we speak into our lives are full of faith because we know God personally, we have made the choice to believe what He says to us, and we understand our authority on the earth. Faith is the substance that creates, and fear is Satan's perversion of faith.

God tells us even demons leave when we speak in faith. The Syrophenician woman followed Jesus, begging for Him to deliver her daughter from a vexing devil. (See Mark 7:26-30.) That woman was not even saved, but she came to Jesus. He did not even answer her or respond to her until He finally tested her by calling her a dog. Jesus said to her, "It is not right to take the children's bread and to cast it to the dogs." Instead of getting offended and leaving in a huff, the woman replied, "Yes Lord, but even the dogs under the table eat the children's crumbs." When she spoke those words, Jesus recognized her great faith and told her that because of what she had said, the devil had gone out of her daughter. Jesus never even saw the child. Jesus never laid a hand on the child. The woman spoke faith-filled words and the devil left. She just needed to get into Jesus' presence and talk with Him. In her dialogue with the God of creation, faith-filled words came out, and her miracle manifested.

Do you need a breakthrough, healing, or deliverance? Go to God's Word. Find out what God says about your circumstance. Enter into dialogue with the God of creation, with Jesus who died to restore dominion to you. Then confess His Word into your circumstance every day. Say it out loud and not just for a day or two, but for a month. Say it every day until the word gets down on the inside of you and until you can see God's word taking care of your situation.

Meditate on that word day and night. Continue to talk to God about it, but don't talk about the problem. Talk about the solution you have found in God's Word. Thank Him. Remind Him, or more accurately remind yourself, of the other times He has performed His word in the earth.

As you search the Scriptures and discuss the will of God with Him, your spirit will become strong in faith. You will see your answer on the inside of you. You will know in your heart of hearts it is coming. And once your spirit can envision your answer, look for it to appear in the natural with the fervent expectation that only God can give. Find someone to get in agreement with you. Speak faith-filled words; then be excited as you expectantly thank and praise God for His goodness.

God has every answer you need. He has given them all to you (2 Peter 1:3). He wants you to use them to walk in wholeness and victory now, in this life. You must put forth the effort to seek, and when you earnestly seek, you shall find. You can no longer always sit around waiting for God to help you. Yes, you can come boldly unto the throne of grace that you may obtain mercy and find grace (favors) to help in time of need (Hebrews 4:16). But you must do your part.

Open your mouth and speak good things. Speak the same things God speaks. Remember, God did not give us all the promises in the Bible just to believe them. He gave them to us so we can boldly say, "The Lord is my helper and I will not fear what man shall do to me." (See Psalm 118:6 and Hebrews 13:6.) He gave them to us so we can open our mouths and claim them.

Open your mouth and claim your health. Open your mouth and claim your financial victory. Open your mouth and claim that restored relationship, that deliverance, that happiness and joy you long for. Open your mouth and fill up your empty place with the good things God has for you. Open your mouth and let faith-filled words spill out.

Believe God. He will never fail you. Believe God loves you. You can trust Him completely.

STUDY GUIDE

1. According to Romans 10:8-10, what does righteousness say?
2. What does the Greek word *sozo* mean?

    a.

    b.

    c.

    d.

    e.

3. What does the Greek word *soteria* mean?

    a.

    b.

    c.

    d.

    e.

    f.

    g.

4. What does it mean to you to know you are delivered now, protected now, preserved now, healed now, and made whole now?

5. It is not enough to just believe. You must open your ________________ and confess your ________________.

6. You must choose to confess God's word over your ________________________.

7. Into what personal life situation do you need to confess God's word right now?

8. You don't just recite words you wish would work. You speak from your knowledge of:

   a.

   b.

9. According to Matthew 8:10, Jesus said the centurion had ________________________ faith.

10. In the situation you listed in number 7 above, do you have great faith, little faith, or no faith?

11. What do you need to do to become strong in faith?

12. Who has every answer you need?

13. What must you do to find the answers you need?

14. Did God give you all the promises in the Bible for you to just believe them? Yes No

15. What do **you** need to do to benefit from God's promises?

LIFE AND DEATH ARE IN YOUR WORDS

A man's belly shall be satisfied with the fruit of his mouth; and with the increase of his lips shall he be filled. Death and life are in the power of the tongue and they that love it shall eat the fruit thereof.

—Proverbs 18:20-21(KJV)

YOU ARE STILL reading. I must assume you have decided to go a bit deeper into what the Bible teaches about the importance of your words. Proverbs has a lot to say about our speech. The book of Proverbs is a collection of wise sayings. These are not promises. These wise sayings are facts that God wants us to understand and apply to our lives.

- Proverbs 12:6 tells us the mouth of the upright shall deliver them.
- Proverbs 12:14 says a man shall be satisfied with good by the fruit of his mouth.

- Proverbs 12:18 says the tongue of the wise is health.
- Proverbs 12:25 says a good word makes the heart glad.
- Proverbs 13:3 tells us that he that keeps his mouth keeps his life and he that talks a lot (my paraphrase) will have destruction.
- Proverbs 15:1-4 tells us a soft answer turns away wrath, that the tongue of the wise uses knowledge correctly, that a wholesome tongue is a tree of life and that a perverse tongue is a breach in the spirit.
- Proverbs 15:23 says we have joy by the answer of our mouth and that a word spoken in due season is good.
- Proverbs 15:26 says the words of the pure are pleasant words.
- Proverbs 16:23-24 tells us the heart of the wise teaches his mouth and adds learning to his lips. It also says pleasant words are…health to the bones.

But Proverbs 18:20-21 really caught my attention. Until my study on the importance of my words, I had always understood Proverbs 18:21 to mean that I could hurt or encourage people by what I said to and about them. And, on a superficial level, it can mean exactly that. But a deeper study of this verse in context reveals much more. I believe Proverbs 18: 20 and 21 are in context and should be studied together.

In verse 20, the Hebrew word for *belly* is *bet en*. It is from an old root word that means to be hollow. Therefore, it must carry that root's meaning into this word which means a body's hollow place; belly and especially the womb; also the bosom or body of anything.[7] The Oxford English

Dictionary defines *hollow* as having a hole or cavity inside; not solid throughout; empty; hungry; without significance; meaningless.[8]

The Hebrew word for *satisfied* is *saba or sabea* and it means to sate, to fill to satisfaction, to be full of, to have plenty of or to be weary of.[9] The Hebrew word for *fruit* is *pery* and it means fruit, bough, reward.[10] The Hebrew word for *mouth* is *peh* and it means the mouth as the means of blowing, particularly speech.[11] The Hebrew word for *increase* is *tebuah* which means income, produce, fruit, gain, increase, revenue. Tebuah comes from the Hebrew root word *bo* which means to bring forth. The Hebrew word for *lips* is *saphah or sepheth* and it means language, lip, speech, talk, words.[12]

In Proverbs 18:21, the Hebrew word for *death* is *maveth* and it means "death (natural or violent), pestilence, ruin."[13] The Hebrew word for life is *chay* and it means alive, living, strong, fresh.[14] The Hebrew word for *power* is *yawd* and it means an open hand indicating power, means, direction, dominion, force.[15] The Hebrew word for *tongue* is *lashon* or *leshonah* and it means the instrument of speech, to blabber, language.[16]

While meditating on these verses, I realized that every place in me that feels hollow or empty can either be satiated and filled to my satisfaction by my words or, by my words, be made weary of ever being filled. I believe I am responsible to speak life into the dead and dying areas of my life; into the holes, the hollow cavities, the empty places and the places where I am not solid. I believe I am to speak life into the dead and dying lives of others; into the aspects of their lives that they see as insignificant and meaningless.

God will take us as deep into His Word as we wish to go. I can wound or encourage people by what I say to and about them, but Proverbs 18:21 tells me much more. It tells me that my speech and my words have the power, dominion, and force to produce pestilence, ruin, and death in my life or to produce strength, life, freshness, or vitality in my life. I can speak life or death into my physical body and into my circumstances. I can speak life or death into my finances and into my relationships. I can speak life or death into my physical body, my soul, or my spirit. I can speak life or death into my calling and into my relationship with God. The choices and the responsibility are mine.

The woman with the issue of blood finally understood this principle. Matthew 9:21 tells us that she "*said within herself…*" She pointed out with words. She called by name (*lego*)[17] to herself that if she was permitted to just touch Jesus' garment she would be whole. She said, "This is what I'm going to do to release my faith" and then she did it. Perhaps she knew what James has told us, that faith without works is dead (James 2:26). This woman did not sit home praying that God would heal her. She had a talk with herself, named her point of faith, and then acted in faith knowing that God is Jehovah Rophe, the God that heals you (Exodus 15:26; Psalm 30:2). She believed God's word was true and that it applied to her. She chose to believe God, and she acted on that belief.

Peter, the disciple who, on more than one occasion, had his foot in his mouth, also finally learned the importance of words. Peter tells us, "For he that will love life, and see good days, let him refrain his tongue from evil, and his lips that they speak no guile" (1 Peter 3:10).

In this verse, the Greek word for *tongue* is *glossa* and it means language.[18] The Greek word for *evil* is *kakos* and it means of a bad nature, of a base, wrong, wicked mode of thinking, feeling, acting, troublesome, injurious, pernicious or baneful.[19] The Greek word translated *speak* is *laleo* and it means to use words in order to declare one's mind and disclose one's thoughts.[20] But I found the most interesting word to be the Greek word translated *guile.* That word is *dolos* and it means deceit, trick.[21] Since I didn't really understand the English definition of *guile*, I looked it up in the Oxford English Dictionary (OED). The OED defines *guile* as treachery, deceit; cunning or sly behavior.[22]

I realized that Peter was essentially telling me that if I want to enjoy life, I must watch my language. I must not speak base (low life) words, or words that are just plain wrong. I must not allow words to slip out that are based on bad attitudes or emotional outbursts or that are destructive (pernicious) or that cause ruin or a curse (baneful).

Do you want to enjoy life? Do you want a good life? Do you want your emptiness to be satisfied? What part of you has been crying out to God for filling or for fulfillment? Perhaps now is the time to change what you speak about that emptiness. Have you been praying for a miracle? Have you been praying for healing, for a financial breakthrough, for a restored relationship, for direction from God? Do you just need to string together a bunch of good days?

What kinds of things are you talking about? Are you talking about how empty you feel, about how long you've been praying for that miracle and about how far away and silent God seems? Are you talking about how bad you feel and about how many things you can't do anymore? Are you talking about how broke you are, about how many bills you have, about how stingy your boss is and about what a rotten job you have? Are you telling everyone who will listen that your spouse left you, or that your kids hate you, or about what awful people you have to work with, or about the dull sermons you endure?

If your body and soul and spirit are weary, you need to look at what has been coming out of your mouth. What have you been speaking into your life? Proverbs 18:20 tells you that what you speak in abundance is what you will be filled with. The choice is yours.

Speech that is contrary to what you want from God negates your prayers. When you pray but then speak contrary to the answer you want, you are being double-minded. And, according to James 1:7, when you are double-minded you will not get anything from the Lord. Perhaps your words are sabotaging the answers to your prayers. Perhaps you need to review what you have been speaking about that thing for which you are waiting. Perhaps your words are keeping your hollow places empty.

It is not too late. Repent right now from the old worldly way of speaking and start speaking God's word into your life. Start using the spiritual laws as God intended. They were created for your use, and they work every time. Make sure you are speaking wisely. Make sure you are speaking the solution; not the problem. Remember, you will live abundantly by the words of God, and you will die by the words of the devil. The choice is yours.

STUDY GUIDE

1. Which of the wise sayings from Proverbs do you need to apply to your life today?

2. What does Proverbs 18:20-21 mean to you?

3. Identify your empty, hollow place. How do you need to change the way you speak about it?

4. Describe a time when you spoke life into your life or into the life of someone else.

5. Describe a time when you spoke death into your life or into the life of someone else.

6. Meditate on 1 Peter 3:10 and then write how it applies to your life.

7. How do you need to change what you have been speaking into your life?

8. Why does saying things that are contrary to what you have prayed for negate your prayers? What verse tells you that?

GOD'S WORD IS MORE POWERFUL THAN YOUR WORDS

It is the Spirit that quickens; the flesh profits nothing: the words that I speak unto you, they are spirit and they are life.

—John 6:63 (KJV)

MY HUSBAND WAS teaching a men's Bible study and was talking about asking God in faith believing for what you want. One man dismissively commented that if that was true, he was going to ask for a new car and a bunch of other things he wanted. Clearly, he had missed the point of James 4:3.

New Age philosophy tells us we should write out and regularly recite affirmations that describe what we want from "the universe." Christians say we should write out and regularly recite our confessions; those things we have asked for and that we believe God will give us. What is the difference? Simply this. God never promised to give us whatever **we** say. He has promised to be faithful to perform **His** word in the earth. We do not get what we want just because we want it; that is a selfish, spoiled, and childish perspective that sounds suspiciously like a verbal temper tantrum. No, God promised to give us what we ask for that is consistent with His will.

But wait, you say. What about Matthew 7:8 where Jesus says "how much more will your Father which is in heaven give good things to them that ask him?" And what about Matthew 21:22 where Jesus again says, "And all things, whatsoever you shall ask in prayer, believing, you shall receive? And what about Psalm 37:4, "He shall give you the desires of your heart" and Mark 11:24, "what things soever you desire, when you pray, believe that you receive them, and you shall have them"? You ask, "True or not?" I submit to you that every verse you just read is absolutely true.

However, Matthew 7:8 is a primary example of why we must study God's Word in context. We must read Matthew 7:8 with its companion verse, Luke 11:10-13 where the thought is completed: "How much more shall your heavenly Father give the Holy Spirit to them that ask Him." Both Matthew and Luke are talking about asking God for those things which we need and specifically about asking God to give us the Holy Spirit. And who of us does not want the Holy Spirit to live and work through us in the wisdom and power that belongs only to Him?

Matthew 21:22 must be understood in context with James 4:3 and 1 John 5:14. James tells us that we ask and do not receive because we ask amiss that we may consume it upon our lusts. John tells us, "And this is the confidence that we have in Him, that if we ask anything according to His will, He hears us: and if we know that He hears us, whatsoever we ask, we know that we have the petitions that we desired of Him." Which of us does not want what God wants for us? Just make sure you have gone to the Word first to see what God Himself has to say about what you are asking for. If what you request is consistent with His revealed Word, ask away in confidence and joy that He will grant your requests.

And then I suggest you meditate on Psalm 37:4, "He shall give you the desires of your heart" and Mark 11:24, "what things soever you desire, when you pray, believe that you receive them, and you shall have them." The Lord asked me how often I had pleaded for something from God that I really wanted; not that I needed for my survival; not that I needed to meet the needs of another; not that I wanted to support the kingdom, but rather for what I wanted just because I really wanted it? I was sorry to admit that many, if not most, of my prayers had been selfish.

As I continued to meditate on Psalm 37:4 and Mark 11:24, I realized that sometimes, many times, I had received my selfish, self-centered desires. Sometimes, like a child with a much-desired toy, the thing I had wanted so much grew old and I soon tired of it. Sometimes, what I received didn't work out like I thought it would. I was disappointed. Sometimes what I asked for ended up costing me much more than I anticipated when I asked for it. And that is when I understood.

God is not obligated to give me what I ask for just because I ask. God has obligated Himself to fulfill His word. I can recite all the positive affirmations I want, but if I am not speaking God's word into my life, the affirmations, while they may occur, are meaningless. I can pray, in faith believing, for all the selfish desires I want, but I am asking amiss and I will not receive them from God. I can order God around all I want, but He knows and responds to my motives.

God may give me my selfish desires to draw me closer to Him or for another reason known only to Him. I may receive what I have been affirming or confessing simply because the spiritual law works every time.

The bottom line is this: God never promised to give me whatever I ask for. God has promised to fulfill His word. God's word, spoken out loud into my life, will never return to Him void but will always accomplish the thing that **God** pleased and it will prosper in the thing to which **God** sent it (Isaiah 55:11).

God is good. He wants me to be blessed so I can be a blessing to others, not so I can consume and waste His blessings on myself. If I truly trust God, I understand He is Jehovah Jireh, my provider, and I know that, because I choose to walk uprightly, He will not withhold any good thing from me (Psalm 34:10, Psalm 84:11).

I will ask in confidence and in faith believing for everything He has promised me in His Word; for everything that is consistent with His Word. That means my motives, the desires of my heart, will also be consistent with His Word. When my motives are consistent with His Word, I know I shall have whatsoever things I desire, when I pray, believing that I receive them. I know God will give me the desires of my heart.

God will indeed give you the desires of your heart whenever your heart lines up with His Word. God loves you. His Word contains everything you need to know to walk in victory and in abundance in this life. You should not be in bondage to the world's system. You are in this world but you are not of this world. Rather, you are a new creation in Christ Jesus unto good works that you should walk in them. God will empower you to walk out His intention for you. And His intention for you includes peace, total life prosperity, and not evil (Jeremiah 29:11).

So, yes what you say is important. It reveals what is really in your heart. And you do get what you say, whether it is good or bad. You get it because God has established spiritual laws which work whether you understand them or not. They work whether you are a Christian or not (Matthew 5:45). But what you say does not happen just because you say it. Saying it is simply how you plant it.

Many ministers will tell you that you must plant your financial seed in order to have a financial breakthrough. God's economy does work on giving in order to receive what you need. However, I submit to you that the Bible does not refer to money as seed. The only thing God has ever called *seed* is the Word...His Word (Matthew 13:19-23; Luke 8:11; 1 Peter 1:23). To have a good harvest, we are expected to plant THE Seed, God's word, in our life.

If you imagine perverse things and speak them (bad seed), you will bring evil to pass (Proverbs 16:30). When you say, "the Lord is my refuge and my fortress: my God; in Him will I trust (good seed)...there shall no evil befall you neither shall any plague come near your house...(Psalm 91:2; 9-11). When you speak God's word (good seed), the angels will hear and will perform it (Psalm 103:20).

However the parable of the sower in Matthew 13 warns us that we must prepare our hearts to receive good seed. You can quote Scripture all day, but if you don't meditate on it and prayerfully ask the Holy Spirit to reveal God's truth to you, you will not understand it and the wicked one will come and catch away that which was sown. You will believe a lie, as Eve did in the Garden, and you will never see the harvest for which you wait and long.

If you or another plants the seed of God's word in your life and you aren't grounded well in the Word, you will enthusiastically receive the word for a while but you will become offended by the attitudes and words of others (trials and persecution that arise because of the word) and you will give up and turn away before your harvest comes. And when the word is sown into your life (by your own words or those of another) and you allow yourself to be distracted by the cares of this world or by the deceitfulness of riches, the word, even as it grows in your life, will be choked out and you will not see the fruit of your harvest.

You must plant God's word by speaking it into your life and into the lives of others. Then you must nurture it. You must ground yourself firmly in the good soil of the Word so your roots grow deep and strong. You must resist every distraction that will cause you to let go of the hope that is before you, the seed of the living Word of God that is at work in you to perfect His plan for you.

Pledge now to search God's Word for His will concerning your needs and the desires of your heart. Go deep. Don't read to find a few words that fit your desire. Search diligently to learn God's heart. Then, pray that. Speak the word of the Living God into your life. Nurture it. Meditate on it. Ask for revelation. And then, having done all, stand in faith believing and watch with joy as God moves heaven and earth on your behalf.

STUDY GUIDE

1. Write Matthew 7:8.

2. Write Matthew 21:22.

3. Write Psalm 37:4.

4. Write Mark 11:24.

5. Read Luke 11:10. What are both Matthew 7:8 and Luke 11:10 referring to?

6. According to James 4:3, we ask and receive not because we ask ____________ that we may ____________.
7. 1 John 5:14 tells us, we can have confidence that if we ask ____________ according to ____________ will, we know that we have what we ____________ of Him.
8. What does Matthew 21:22 mean in conjunction with James 4:3 and 1 John 5:14?

9. Indicate whether the following verses are True or False: _____ Matthew 7:8; _____ Matthew 21:22; _____ Ps 37:4; _____ Mark 11:24.
10. God never promised to give me what _____ say. He has promised to be faithful to perform _____ word in the earth and to give us what is consistent with _______.
11. God is _________ to give me what I ask for just because I ask. God has obligated Himself to _________ Word.
12. God's word spoken out loud into my life, will ______ return to Him void but will ______ accomplish the thing that ______ pleased and it will prosper in the thing to which ______ has sent it (Isaiah 55:11).
13. God is good. He wants me to be blessed so I can be a _________ to _________ not so I can _________ and _________ His blessings on myself.
14. God will give me the desires of my heart whenever my heart ____________ with _____ Word.
15. The only thing God ever called "seed" is _______ (Matthew 13:19-23; Luke 8:11; 1 Peter 1:12).

16. We must prepare our ______________ to receive good seed.

17. We plant God's word by ______________ it into our life and into the lives of others. We must ______________ ourselves firmly in the good soil of the ______________ so our roots grow deep and strong and we must ______________ every distraction that will cause us to let go of the ______________ that is before us—the seed of the living Word of God that is at work in us to perfect His plan for each of us.

18. What do you need to do now to nurture, water, and tend the seed?

19. Identify a time when you have trusted your own words more than God's word. What was the result?

20. Ask the Lord to show you how you need to apply His word to a problematic situation in your life.

SEEDTIME AND HARVEST

While the earth remaineth, seedtime and harvest, and cold and heat, and summer and winter, and day and night shall not cease.

—Genesis 8:22 (KJV)

Hear the parable of the sower. When anyone hears the word of the kingdom, and does not understand it, the wicked one comes and takes that which was sown in his heart. This is the person who received seed by the wayside.

But people that receive the seed in stony places, are the ones that hear the word, and receive it with joy; yet are not themselves rooted, but only endure for a while: for when tribulation or persecution comes because of the word, they are eventually offended.

Whoever receives seed in with the thorns is the one that hears the word; and the care of this world, and the deceitfulness of riches, choke the word and he or she becomes unfruitful.

But the one that receives seed into the good ground is the one that hears the word, and understands it; which also

> *bears fruit and brings forth some one hundred fold, some sixty, some thirty.*
>
> —Matthew 13:18-26 [my paraphrase]

YOU HAVE PLANTED God's word in your heart. You have tilled the soil of your heart, and it received the word with joy. You are being watchful that you are not offended by the attitudes, words, and actions of others. You are not distracted by the cares of this life or by the deceitfulness of wealth. You are standing in faith believing that God is answering your prayer. And, while you stand, you can meditate on God's plan concerning seed time and harvest.

The first two gifts God gave to man are found in the first chapter of Genesis. God's first gift to man was dominion over all the earth and over everything in it (Genesis 1:26). God's second gift to man was seeding seed (Genesis 1:29). Most Bibles translate the Hebrew word used here (*za ra zera*) as herb-bearing seed. The proper translation is herb or grass-seeding seed or sowing seed. What does that mean to us?

God's plan was never that we live our lives by default. Rather, we are to take control; to take dominion. We do that by planting our seed. We take dominion by taking God's second gift, in its simplest form, and using this spiritual principle to plant His Word into our lives and, in a wider sense, into the earth.

How does sowing seed work? I live in the Midwest. Whenever I leave the little town in which I live, I see farmland. Even when farmers are not planting seed, they are tilling the ground, preparing it to receive the seed. Then, in the spring they plant the sowing seed. It is the best seed. They don't plant leftover seed; they use good seed. When the sowing seed is planted, the farmer does not just sit around and rest until harvest time. Some farmers water the seed (irrigate), some check with local agricultural centers to see what this year's pests are and then spray pesticide and herbicide, some fertilize. All are watchful for things external to the seed that may affect the harvest.

I don't know of any farmer who goes out and worries over the seed he's planted. He may worry about whether it will rain or whether wind, hail, or bugs will destroy his crop. But I've never heard a farmer talking about whether or not the seed he just planted is growing or doubt he will have a harvest because "you just never know whether seed will grow." He simply waits and watches it grow. He may pray for rain and for God to bless his crop, but he understands he cannot make it grow and mature faster than God intends. He waits.

Suppose one day the farmer went to his field a week or two after planting and said, "I don't see any crop here. This seed isn't working. It's not growing. I must have done something wrong. I'll never get this right. At this rate, I'll never get my harvest. I'd better start over." So he plows up his field and replants some more good seed. After a few weeks, he goes back to his field and, not seeing much growth, he plows up his crop again. Will this farmer ever get his harvest? No. Is it the seed's fault? No, he planted good seed. He was impatient, and he spoke that which was perverse. He should have said, "I don't see a thing. But I know I've planted good seed. I know I prepared the soil well. I know the seed is growing even though I can't see it and that I will have my harvest on time. God is good; He will perfect His Word. The seed is growing. I speak life and health to my seed."

Or, suppose a farmer waits until September to plant his field. He knows he needs a harvest by October, so he plants good seed in September. Will he have a good harvest when he needs it? No. Is it because the seed did not work? No, it is because the farmer was not attentive. Or perhaps he wanted a miracle preferring to take the easy way rather than to walk in divine blessing, diligently living and working according to what he knew was true and necessary.

Just like the farmer, you will not receive your harvest on time if you neglect to plant faith-filled words in your life. A crisis is not a good time to start planting good seed.

As some of you look at the garden of your heart, you see a few flowers and a lot of weeds all mixed together, nothing really planned, it all just happened. That is inattentiveness. That is living by default. That mixture of flowers and weeds happened because you have not been planting anything and you have not been weeding your garden. The junk of other people's lives has trashed parts of your life (Matthew 13:25-26). It is no wonder your speech and your prayers don't agree. You must speak God's word into your life and intercede for others by teaching them and by reminding God of His promises regarding that person.

And understand that you don't remind God so He remembers what He promised. You speak His word into your situation and you find your faith is increasing each time you "remind" God of His promises. Somehow, when you talk things over with God, His word begins to make sense to you. When you "remind" God of what His Word says, as you meditate on it, it starts to make sense to you. You start to understand how it applies to you and to your situation. As you "remind" God of His word, you begin to expect Him to meet your need. The word you have been speaking begins to grow inside you and eventually, you will have your harvest. God will meet your need.

Seed time and harvest are here to stay. It's one of God's laws. It works in the natural world and it works in the spirit world. It works for sinners and it works for saints.

Genesis 8:22 says, "While the earth remains, seedtime and harvest, and cold and heat, and summer and winter and day and night shall not cease" (NKJ). God gives us examples in the physical world to explain spiritual laws; for example, conception and birth (James 1), families, and here, farming.

Seedtime and harvest is one of the ways God continues to work in the earth. We must plant good seed, and we must wait for the harvest. As we wait, we don't plow up our seed by speaking words of doubt and unbelief. We don't stomp on our seed by constantly speaking the problems we face. We pray God's will concerning our situation in faith believing that He is faithful to perform His word, and then we water that seed with words of faith and praise and thanksgiving. In due time, we shall receive our harvest.

So how much faith do we need? Not much. Jesus tells us all it takes is faith as small as a grain of mustard seed. We can have great faith, but if we never speak to our problem, it will stay right where it is. However, when we have even a tiny speck of faith, and we speak that tiny bit of faith to our problem, the problem will obey us (Luke 17:6).

How much clearer and more direct does Jesus need to be? When we don't get what we need, it is either because we don't have any faith or because we are just sitting around expecting God to take care of everything for us. No. We are to go to God's word and find out what He says. Then, we make a quality decision to believe God. Finally, into our situation we speak God's word filled with our own faith in His faithfulness. And we wait, content in Jesus with joyful hearts full of thanksgiving, for the wonder of our lives in Christ.

Jesus tells us in Mark that the kingdom of God works on the principle of seedtime and harvest. We have not planted the corruptible seed of the world. We have planted incorruptible seed, God's word, by speaking it into our situation.

While we rest in Jesus, the seed springs and grows up. We don't know how but it does. The world doesn't understand how, but our seed still grows. And when the fullness of time has come, we will have our harvest (Mark 4:26-29).

Jesus applies this principle in another kind of situation. The bad seeds we plant by our words will also produce a harvest in our lives. Peter denied Jesus three times. Three times he said he was not one of Jesus' followers and that he did not know Jesus. After Jesus died and was resurrected, He showed Himself to the disciples. Peter was there. They ate together, and after dinner, Jesus asked Peter three times if he loved Him (John 21:15-19). Jesus understood that Peter needed to publicly acknowledge and affirm his love for Jesus three times to, in effect, nullify his three denials. Because of His great love for Peter, Jesus made sure Peter spoke this truth into his life before Jesus left this earth. He did not allow Peter to remain in his denial.

We reap what we sow (Galatians 6:7). If you don't like the harvest in your life, look to the seed you have been planting with your words. Dig up that field and start planting good seed.

Even if you have spoken doubt and unbelief into your situation, you can change it right now. Ask the Holy Spirit to reveal and to bring to your remembrance all the words of doubt and unbelief that you have been speaking into your situation. Ask for a revelation of all the unscriptural words others have spoken into your life that you have accepted as truth. Regardless of their source, rebuke all the words of doubt and unbelief and cast them down (2 Corinthians 10:5). Call them subject to the authority of the Word of the Living God. Tell them, in Jesus name, that they have no power or authority in your life from this day forward. Then, replace them by speaking the Word of God into that situation. Don't wait; do it right now.

I believe speaking the words of God in faith is the most powerful weapon in the world of the Spirit. Satan is a spirit being, but he is not powerful enough to overcome the faith-filled word of God. The words you speak are more important to you than to anyone else; they affect you more than they affect anyone else. Begin speaking God's words right now.

STUDY GUIDE

1. While the earth remains, ________________ and ________________ and cold and heat and summer and winter and day and night shall not cease (Genesis 8:22).
2. The first two gifts God gave to man are ____________ (Genesis 1:26) and ______________ seed (Genesis 1:29).
3. Bearing (za ra) seed is ______________ seed.
4. God's plan was never that we live our lives by default, but rather that we take ______________; that we take dominion.
5. We take dominion of our lives and, in a larger sense, of our world by planting the ____________ in our hearts.
6. A person who receives seed by the wayside does not ______________ it and Satan takes it out of her heart.
7. A person who receives seed in stony places hears the word and receives it with ______________ but he is eventually ______________.
8. The thorns that choke the word are ________________ and ____________________________________.
9. When the word is received in good ground it is ______________ and it bears ______________.
10. After a farmer plants his seed he ______________ and watches it grow.
11. A farmer who prepares his soil and plants good seed but who tills everything up and starts over every few days because he doesn't see immediate results will ______________ get his harvest.

12. A farmer who is inattentive and who does not plant his seed on time or who wanted a miracle and never planted his seed at all will ____________ get his harvest.

13. A ____________ is not a good time to start planting God's word in your heart.

14. When you live by default, you are inattentive: you do not ____________ the good seed and you do not ____________ the weeds other people have planted in your life.

15. List weeds (unscriptural words) that others have planted in your heart that you have not removed.

16. You must plant ____________, ____________ and ____________ for the harvest.

17. You can plow up your good seeds by speaking words of ____________ and ____________.

18. How much faith do you need? ____________

19. What does Luke 17:6 say you must do when you use your faith? ____________

20. When you don't get what you need, it is either because you don't have ____________ faith or because you are just sitting around ____________ ____________ to take care of everything for you.

21. The steps to receiving what you need are:

    a. Go to ________ word and find out what __________ says.

    b. Make a quality decision to ________________.

c. ____________ God's word filled with our ____________ in ____________ faithfulness into our situation.

d. ____________ with joyful hearts full of thanksgiving.

22. According to Mark 4:26-29, the kingdom of God works on the principle of ____________ and ____________.

23. According to Galatians 6:7 you will ____________ what you ____________.

24. 2 Corinthians 10:5 applies to all your words of ____________ and ____________ as well as to the unscriptural words ____________ have spoken into your life.

CALLING THINGS THAT ARE NOT AS THOUGH THEY WERE

(As it is written, I have made you a father of many nations,) before him whom he believed, even God, who quickeneth the dead, and calleth those things which be not as though they were.

—Romans 4:17.(KJV)

But God hath chosen the foolish things of the world to confound the wise; and God hath chosen the weak things of the world to confound the things which are mighty; and base things of the world, and things which are despised, hath God chosen, and yea ***things which are not, to bring to nought things that are****: that no flesh should glory in his presence.*

—1 Corinthians 1:27-29. (KJV)[Emphasis added]

I REMEMBER WHEN I first heard that I was to claim that I was healed; I was sicker than I had been in a long, long time. I tried to say I was healed, but I felt (and believed) I was lying. It seemed like such an obvious lie; how could it be otherwise? I was sick, but I was saying I was healed. I had a fever, and I couldn't get out of bed, but I was saying I was healed. Then God gave me a revelation about His way of doing things.

I saw that in Genesis 1:1-2 God saw darkness. Darkness was pre-creation reality. So from the midst of that reality of darkness, God spoke light. Then God saw light. When there was no firmament in the middle of the waters, God said "let there be a firmament" and then it was so. And day after day during the creation of our earth, God saw one reality but spoke another into existence. And all that He spoke into existence was good. He used words filled with His faith to speak His wonderful, diverse, magnificent creation into existence. It did not matter what He saw. What mattered was what He spoke.

When I asked for confirmation of this revelation, God showed me Romans 4:17, "...God, who quickens the dead and calls those things which be not as though they were" (more literally, who makes alive the lifeless and calls that forth). So, I understood that God calls things that are not as though they are and that I, created in His image and likeness, do the same whenever I speak His word and His will into the situations of my life.

This is God's way of doing things. It does not make sense to the world's system. We do not understand how it works or why it works other than that it is God's way. And that makes it good.

As with all of life, Satan cannot create so he corrupts. And Satan has taken God's way of creating good and corrupted it by deceiving humans into believing what they say does not matter. He encourages us to speak the world's words of doubt and frustration and anger and futility and fear into our lives. What we say still creates but in the world system, controlled by the deceiver, we now can create evil and cause those things that steal, kill, and destroy to enter our lives.

Such darkness the deceiver brings. How empowering to know the light and love of Jesus transcends everything the deceiver tries to trick us into claiming. All we are required to do is to change how we talk. All we are required to do is to believe God and to speak His words into our lives.

We have another example of God calling things that did not exist as though they did exist. Abram had no children. God entered into a covenant with Abram and told him he would be a father of many nations. God even changed Abram's name to Abraham, father of a great multitude or father of many nations, and Sarai's name to Sarah, mother of nations. God made sure every time anyone said Abraham's or Sarah's name they spoke the promise into their lives. God made sure everyone in Abraham's and Sarah's sphere of influence cooperated in calling into existence something that was not yet reality.

God went even further and gave Abraham a visual aid to help him. God told Abraham (then Abram) to look into the heavens. There were no city lights to dim the starry night. Abraham could clearly see all the multitude of stars in the heavens. God told Abram that his offspring would be as the stars in number. God saw it and spoke it before it was reality, and He gave Abram something to look at that would reinforce the promise until he actually experienced the promise. Abraham did not weaken when he saw his natural weakness; he grew strong as he gave praise and glory to God (Romans 4:19-22).

God even underscored this spiritual law by giving us two New Testament examples. Luke 1 tells the story of Zachariah, a righteous man, who, in the face of reality, did not have faith to believe God's word; even when it was delivered to him by an angel. The angel told Zachariah he and his wife Elizabeth would have a child. But not only was Elizabeth barren, both Zachariah and Elizabeth were old.

When the angel told Zachariah that his prayer for a child had been heard and that Elizabeth would have a child, Zachariah doubted and questioned the angel.

The angel had called things that are not as though they were when he spoke God's message to Zachariah. Because Zachariah did not believe God's word spoken by the angel (Luke 1:20), the angel had to make him mute. If Zachariah had been able to talk, his words of doubt and unbelief would have prevented the miracle. His words would have kept God's plan from manifesting.

Zachariah was not able to speak again until after the child was born and named. When God's plan was complete, when there was no danger that he would ruin the plan, Zachariah was again able to speak.

In contrast, we are told of Mary, the mother of Christ (Luke 1:26-38). Mary was an unmarried virgin. An angel appeared to her and told her she would conceive and bear Jesus, who would be called the Son of the Highest and that there would be no end of His kingdom. The angel again called things that were not as though they were when he spoke God's message to Mary.

Although Mary did not understand how such things could be and questioned the angel, her questions were apparently not based in any doubt or disbelief of God's word. She was only trying to understand how it would happen. The angel simply told her that with God nothing shall be impossible (Luke 1:37). Mary's response was one of belief and acceptance. She spoke words of faith and trust (Luke 1:46-55). Mary was not made mute. God knew she would not stop His plan by speaking doubt and unbelief into her circumstance or by refusing to accept God's word as a definitive statement of His will.

Mary received God's word into herself. As she meditated on the word, that Word (Jesus), the incorruptible seed (1 Peter 1:23) was physically conceived in her. The Word became flesh (John 1:14). We don't understand how; Mary did not understand how. We do know that God always releases sufficient faith as He speaks His words to cause them to come to pass, but we, like Mary, must receive His word in faith and allow it to remain in us nurtured by our own words of faith, praise, and thanksgiving.

We also know from Genesis 3:15 that God prophesied Jesus would defeat Satan. Throughout the centuries, God had the prophets speak of Jesus coming and His final victory over Satan. Satan tried to stop His coming. He tried to pollute the human race. He tried to kill the prophets, those men of God who spoke the Word of God into the world. Satan even tried to corrupt Jesus. But God's word is true, and He causes it to accomplish that to which He has sent it.

So, do you believe God? Adam and Eve chose to believe the lie instead of believing God. Do you believe God's word is true? If you believe God's word is true, then it will pre-empt the reality of your life. If you believe God, you have every right to call things that are not as though they are by saying the same thing about them that God does. You call things that are not as though they are every time you speak God's word into your life, regardless of what you see or feel and regardless of what others tell you. I believe God expects you to claim your future and to fervently expect that future to be abundantly satisfying.

According to Philippians 4:19, God shall supply all your need according to his riches in glory by Christ Jesus. Claim it and speak it into your life in faith believing; regardless of your circumstances.

According to Luke 6:38, when you give, it shall be given unto you: good measure, pressed down, shaken together, and running over, shall men given into your bosom. For with the same measure that you measure, it shall be measured to you again. Jesus is repeating in Luke what God said in Malachi 3:10-11.

Do you have a financial need? You must believe this verse and give yourself out of debt and into prosperity. Just check your motives. You don't give out of fear and desperation. And you don't give to just anybody or to just any ministry. You give because you understand and trust God's way of doing things. You give where God tells you to give, and you give what God tells you to give because you know who your provider is and because you trust Him to meet your needs. God loves a cheerful giver. God blesses you to be a blessing to others.

Are you concerned about the economy? Psalms 1:1-3 tells us God blesses the person whose delight is in the law of the Lord; the one who meditates on God's word day and night. God tells us that such a person will prosper regardless of other circumstances because of where that person is planted. Where are you planted? Speak these words into your circumstances. God's words are life and health.

1 Peter 2:24 tells us we have already been healed by the stripes that were cut into Jesus' body. Do you believe God's word? Is God a man that He should lie and apply this truth to everyone else except you? No. Do you need healing? Claim this truth and speak it into your reality. God's truth preempts reality every time.

Do you have enemies all around you? Isaiah 54:17 tells you no weapon formed against you shall prosper; and every tongue that shall come against you in judgment you shall condemn. God says this is the heritage of the servants of the Lord and their righteousness is of Him. Believe God's word applies to you. Speak these words of life into your circumstance.

Are these truths operating in your life? If not, why not? Are you thinking these verses don't apply to you; that it just isn't God's will for your life? If so, those are lies straight from Satan's mind to your heart and you are deceived. The Word of God **is** the will of God. If you are speaking anything less, you are speaking doubt and unbelief and are being deceived by the evil one.

But make no mistake. God's word will not happen in your life just because it is God's will. It is God's will that no one shall perish but that all shall come to repentance. Is everyone going to heaven? No. God lets you choose. You choose eternal life by your words, and you choose God's best for your life by your words.

One final note concerning calling things which are not as though they were, and it is important. Do not call things that are as though they were not. Abraham did NOT say, "I'm not old and Sarah's not old. Thank you God that Sarah and I are not old anymore." If he had said those things Abraham would have been lying, and God will not bless a lie. Rather Abraham said, "I'm the father of many nations"...every time he said his name. And Abraham called Sarah the mother of nations every time he said her name. Abraham called it the way God called it. He used the same words God used because he had faith that God would perform His word.

If you are believing to be healed, don't say, "I'm fine; nothing is wrong with me." Instead say, "I've got a healing going on. By Jesus' stripes I have already been healed."

If you need a financial breakthrough don't say, "I'm rich" and start spending money you don't have to live a lifestyle you can't yet afford. Say, "It is God that gives me power to get wealth" (Deuteronomy 8:18). Say, "Because I hear and obey the voice of the Lord my God, His blessings overtake me" (Deuteronomy 28:1-2). Say, "My God supplies all my needs according to his riches in glory in Christ Jesus" (Philippians 4:19).

If you are getting forgetful, stop claiming forgetfulness and say instead, "I have the mind of Christ" (1 Corinthians 2:16) and "God has not given me the spirit of fear, but of power, and of love and of a sound mind" (2 Timothy 1:7).

Never again focus on what is wrong with your life. Focus instead on what God says about your circumstance. Speak God's word into your situation and keep talking about what God is accomplishing on your behalf. Even when you don't see your situation getting better keep your focus on God's word. Call those things which are not now your reality as though they were your reality. Your current reality is temporary because it exists in the temporal world. But God's word is spirit and it is life and it does not change. God's word is the Truth, and it will change your circumstances.

STUDY GUIDE

1. When did God first demonstrate calling things that are not as though they were?

2. God spoke creation into existence by using __________ filled words.

3. I can create either ______________ or ______________ by my words.

4. List several examples of God calling things that did not exist as though they did exist.

5. According to Romans 4:19-22, how did Abraham stay strong in his faith?

6. Explain in your own words the difference between the responses of Zacharias and Jesus' mother, Mary when God called something into their lives that did not then exist.

7. What verse tells you that with God nothing shall be impossible? ____________________

8. How do you receive God's word into yourself?

9. What does God tell you about your finances?

10. What does God tell you about healing?

11. Will God provide for you? Yes No

12. How do you know?

13. Will God protect you? Yes No

14. How do you know?

15. God's word will not happen in your life just because it is God's will. You must ____________ it by your ____________.

16. Identify an area of your life where you need to call things that are not as though they are.

YOU WILL GIVE ACCOUNT OF WHAT YOU SAY

A good man out of the good treasure of the heart brings forth good things: and an evil man out of the evil treasure brings forth evil things.
But I say unto you, That every idle word that men shall speak they shall give account thereof in the day of judgment. For by your words you shall be justified and by your words you shall be condemned.

—Matthew 12:35-37 [my paraphrase]

AS I BEGAN my study on the importance of my words, my mind was captivated by these words, spoken by Jesus as He talked with the Pharisees. The Pharisees had just accused Jesus of being empowered by Beelzebub, the prince of the devils. Jesus began to reason with them as only Jesus can. He ended by telling them that our mouths speak out of what is in our heart; that we speak good from our hearts and we speak evil from our hearts.

The Greek word translated in Matthew 12:35 as *good* is *agathos* and it means, "of a good constitution or nature;

useful, salutary, good, pleasant, agreeable, joyful, happy, excellent, distinguished, upright, honorable."[23] The Greek word translated here as *evil* is *ponayros* and it means, "1) full of labours, annoyances, hardships...bringing toils, annoyances, perils..., causing pain and trouble, 2) bad, of a bad nature or condition, 3a)in a physical sense: diseased or blind 3b) in an ethical sense: evil wicked, bad."[24]

Then Jesus spoke the words of Matthew 12:36 and 37. Jesus says that we will give account of every idle word we speak and that our account will either justify or condemn us. The Greek word for *idle* is *argos* and it means "1) free from labour; at leisure 2) lazy, shunning the labor which one ought to perform, inactive, unemployed."[25] When I speak carelessly or thoughtlessly, I am uttering idle words. When I talk just to talk, that is with no purpose, I am in great danger of speaking idle words. In the multitude of words there wants not sin, but he that refrains his lips is wise (Proverbs 10:19).

The Greek word translated *word* in verse 36 is *rhema* and it means, "that which has been uttered by the living voice... what one has said."[26] It is the subject matter of the word or the thing which is spoken about.[27] And, interestingly, the word translated *account* in Matthew 12:36 and the word translated *words* in Matthew 12:37 are the same Greek word, *logos*. *Logos* means "a word spoken by a living voice [that] embodies a conception or idea...reason.... account, i.e. answer or explanation in reference to judgment..."[28] It is the expression of thought.[29]

I believe Jesus is telling us, as directly as He can, that we will eventually be required to explain every lazy, careless, thoughtless word we have spoken. And our reason for speaking it will either justify (*dikaioo* "to declare or pronounce one to be just, righteous, or such as he ought to be"[30]) or condemn us (*katadikazo*, "to give judgment against, to pronounce guilty."[31])

As I read and meditated on these words of Jesus within the context of discovering the importance of the words I speak, I understood that my words are important because, unless I am a liar, my spoken words reveal what I have allowed to be planted in my heart. I might not even believe it, but it is there either because I have intentionally placed it there or because I have allowed it to grow there by default.

I realized I intentionally place good things in my heart when I read and memorize God's Word, when I engage in helpful, loving conversations, when I choose to limit what T.V. programs and what movies I watch, when I choose to listen to Christian or other sacred music rather than the music of the world. I choose to plant good seed when I choose to read Christian or other wholesome novels rather than the world's violence and sex-filled fiction, and when I choose to limit what internet sites I visit. And I realized I help nourish the good seed I have planted when I choose to meditate on what is true and just and of good report (Philippians 4:8) rather than on all the negative things that come at me on a daily basis.

I realized I have allowed many seeds to grow by default. Some are seeds planted by others to whom I have carelessly exposed myself. Perhaps some evil seeds have been planted by family or friends or educators who have spoken false words or words of criticism or fear or lack into my life. And I nourish the evil seeds when I choose to meditate on them, worry about them, and accept them as a replacement for God's truth in my life. I nourish evil seeds when I choose to see myself as I think others see me rather than believing I am who God sees me to be.

I realized I did not want to give account of much of what I have spoken. All those words full of labor, annoyances and hardship, pain and trouble, sickness and lack. All those words spoken in frustration, anger, loneliness, and insecurity. How many words have I spoken in ignorance and just plain laziness? How many times have my words defiled me (Mark 7:15-23)?

Hosea 4:6 says, "My people are destroyed for lack of knowledge..." How many good things in my own life have I destroyed by my words? How much damage and destruction have my words wrecked in the lives of my family, my friends, and my co-workers? I am not thinking now of intentionally mean words, but of thoughtless, careless, or lazy words spoken because I did not understand the power of my words or my responsibility to use words to further God's kingdom on earth?

But now, praise God, I know and it is my responsibility to place good things in my heart. It is my responsibility to purposefully speak good things into my own life and into the lives of others. I have repented of the old worldly way of speaking. I have rejected the deception.

And as only God can orchestrate, I don't need to work at throwing off the world's language. I simply concentrate and focus on moving into Jesus. And as I move further into Jesus, as I become like Him, the old ways and the old idle words will become non-operative in my life. I will become fluent in the language of heaven; a language full of grace and honor, of power and love, of understanding and forgiveness. I will become holy as He is holy.

Purpose with me that, from this day forward, you will guard your speech. Make a quality decision right now that you will only speak good things into your life, into the lives of those with whom you are in relationship, and into the lives of those God sends to you.

STUDY GUIDE

1. A good man out of the ________________ of the ____________ brings forth good things; and an evil man out of the ______________________ brings forth evil things (Matthew 12:35).
   - "Good" means: ________________________________

     ____
   - "Evil" means: 1) in a physical sense: __________

     2) in an ethical sense: ___________________.
2. But I say unto you that ______________ word that men shall speak they shall give account of in the Day of Judgment. For by your ______________ you shall be justified and by your ______________ you shall be condemned. (Matthew 12:36-37).
   - "Idle" means ______________________________
   - "_______________" means the subject matter of the spoken word and
   - "_______________" means the thought, idea or reason behind what is spoken.
3. My spoken words are important because they reveal what I have allowed ________________________

   ____.
4. The prospect of giving account for every idle word that I have spoken ______________________________

   ____.
5. How are good things planted in the heart?

6. How is the good seed that has been planted, nourished?

7. How is bad or evil seed planted and nourished?

8. How do we allow seed to grow by default?

9. How will you get rid of the world's language?

DON'T SABOTAGE YOUR LIFE BY YOUR WORDS

Therefore take no thought, saying, What shall we eat? or, What shall we drink? or, Wherewithal shall we be clothed?

—Matthew 6:31 (KJV)

Not that which goeth into the mouth defileth a man; but that which cometh out of the mouth, this defiles a man.

—Matthew 15:11(KJV)

If any man among you seem to be religious and bridleth not his tongue, but deceiveth his own heart, this man's religion is vain.

—James 1:26 (KJV)

GOD HAS REVEALED much about what we say. In fact, God gives us more instruction about our speech than He gives us about money or sex or power. God has given us many examples of what we should say and of what not to say.

Matthew 6:31 is one example of what not to say. Applying the principles already studied here, I believe God has instructed us to instead say, "My God shall supply all my needs according to His riches in glory in Christ Jesus." The world says some people look at every glass as half full while others look at every glass as half empty. Speaking faith-filled words goes beyond the world's understanding.

When we speak faith-filled words, we speak God's word into our situation even as we look at the glass of our circumstances. God's way is for us to see the glass either half empty or half full and still to call it full and overflowing; to see weakness and to say strength; to see sickness and to say health; to see brokenness and to call it whole; to see terror and to speak peace. By our words we are justified, and by our words we are condemned.

When I understood that I was actually defiled by my words (Matthew 15:11), I began to change how I talked. When I realized the real message of James 1:26 is that the uncontrolled power of my words will destroy and that I must therefore operate within God's rules for my speech, I began to pray for wisdom and understanding. I asked the Holy Spirit to teach me how to create the life God wanted for me by using words as He intended; to create that which is good, and perfect and acceptable for His glory and honor.

And, as I began to change how I talked, I found I was changing how I thought. My heart changed, and my soul started to line up with my regenerated spirit. It became easier to recognize when the world, the flesh, or the devil was trying to influence my circumstances. I became less critical and less negative. I was less easily offended. God's nature became my nature as I saw good in others. I no longer liked most movies and T.V. shows. I found it uncomfortable to listen to gossip. I worried less. I smiled more.

I still worked as hard and was still stressed but the stress transitioned from emotional and mental stress that depressed me and wore me out to the physical stress needed to energize a multi-tasking, fast-paced lifestyle. I no longer dreaded mornings. Instead, I learned to speak blessing, protection and successful service into each day. I talked to God more; I thanked Him more; I appreciated Him more; I was able to feel His love more.

I no longer say or even think, "maybe God doesn't mean this promise for me." All the promises in the Bible are meant for me. One of my favorite songs is, "Yes and Amen" as sung by Hillsongs. It is based on 2 Corinthians 1:20: "For all the promises of God in Him are yes and in Him amen, unto the glory of God by us." I know God is no respecter of persons (Acts 10:34, Romans 2:11, Ephesians 6:9). What I find in context in God's Word does apply to me regardless of my circumstances. God wrote it for me to read and to understand; to believe and to act upon. I am less likely now to be moved by what I see. I have chosen to believe God.

I no longer sabotage my life by speaking words of doubt and unbelief. Although I still occasionally let such words slip out, I am usually quick to recognize them as deception and cast them down as imaginations that are trying to exalt themselves above God's word. I choose to exercise dominion over my words by making them subject to my regenerated spirit man.

My challenge now is not so much correcting negative, ungodly speech. Rather, it is to intentionally speak God's word into my life. I love studying and teaching God's Word. My desire is to go deeper and deeper into His wisdom and to understand His methods and ways and then to learn to apply them. And, in general, I am more comfortable thinking than I am talking; someone has said I am more cerebral than verbal.

But lately when I have been faced with a problem, God has challenged me to take time to take dominion over the situation and intentionally speak His words into it.

Sometimes I am quick to speak life and health; sometimes, intending to do it later, I wait. Right now, I am making a quality decision to change that.

Ask God what you need to do to take dominion over your life and the forces that come against you. God has not given you the spirit of fear, but of power and love and a sound mind (2 Timothy 1:7). Take dominion over whatever involves fear, lack, emptiness, or bondage. Go to His Word and find His answers to your situations. Then open your mouth and speak God's words. Not just once or twice but multiple times each day until you see His salvation on the inside of you. Your victory is just around the corner, and it sounds like your voice because it is you that is calling it forth.

STUDY GUIDE

1. What defiles you?

2. How will the knowledge of what defiles you change the way you talk?

3. According to Matthew 6:31 what should you NOT say?

4. What should you say instead?

5. What both justifies you and condemns you?

6. According to this chapter, what is the real message of James 1:26?

7. In what area of your life do you need to take dominion?

8. Search the Bible today and tomorrow for what God says about that situation. Write the verses and references. Meditate on them. Speak them (out loud) into your situation every day for one month or longer; until they get into your heart.

CONCLUSION

WORDS CAN DESTROY you or they can transform you because words, your words or the words of another, produce either faith or fear. Your words come from your heart. What is in your heart is what you have sowed and what you have allowed others to sow there.

The faith that is in your heart and in your mouth will create good things in abundance in your life; the fear that is there will destroy. You only need a little faith, but you can destroy your faith by praying and talking about the problem instead of praying and speaking the Word. Faith comes by hearing; so does fear.

Using your words to speak the Word of God into your life is a process of building God's word into your spirit. You must do it intentionally and continually, then, in the fullness of time, God's word will manifest in your life. You can speak the problem and get fear and more of the same problem, or you can speak the promises with praise and glory to God and get the "soteria" you need. You can listen to others speak their problems and watch as they get more of the same, or you can teach them to guard their lips and to speak God's truth rather than continuing to talk about their reality.

You are here, in this country, at this time in history to be a witness of God's love. You are here to demonstrate to everyone in your sphere of influence that God loves them and that He wants to bless them.

You are here to demonstrate the dominion Jesus gave back to man. Learn to walk in it for Jesus' sake and to glorify the Father. God is good. The world needs the good news. It needs to see the sick healed and those in bondage set free. It needs to see provision for the widows and orphans. It needs to see kindness toward those in prison. The lost need to see the victory that comes from doing things God's way.

You can't reach out to others if you are full of lack and emptiness. You can't be a witness to the gospel if you are beaten and bruised by the world's system.

Now is the time. You are here for such a time as this. You have been given much and much is required of you. Demonstrate what it means to believe God.

The choice is yours to make today, now. The choice is yours to make every day and in every situation throughout each day.

"The Word is nigh thee, even in thy mouth and in thy heart" (Romans 10:8 KJV). Speak it and change your life.

POST SCRIPT

IF YOU ARE a believer who has allowed sin to separate you from God, simply confess your sin. God says in 1 John 1:9 that if we confess our sin, He is faithful and just to forgive our sin and to cleanse us from all unrighteousness. Just talk with God. Even when you turned from Him, He never left you. He's just waiting for you to turn around and come back to Him. Trust Him. He loves you.

If you have never entered into relationship with Jesus, all you need to do is to confess with your mouth that Jesus is your Lord and believe in your heart that God has raised Jesus from the dead. When you do that, you are saved (Romans 10:9-10). For God so loved the world that He gave His only begotten Son (that's Jesus) that whosoever (that's you) believes in Him should not perish but should have everlasting life (John 3:16). God is not trying to keep people out of heaven. He has made it easy to know that you have eternal life.

Now you need to grow in Him. That means you need to learn how He thinks and how He acts, and then do the same. You need to talk with Him every day, just like you talk to your other friends. And you need to take time to listen to Him; He will talk to your spirit.

Read the Bible. He also talks to you through the written Word. The Bible is God speaking to *you*. It is God telling *you* the stories of faith, failure, and redemption. It contains what God wants to say to *you*. Nothing He tells you in your spirit will be different from what He says in the Bible.

And finally, find a good church or Bible study, one that doesn't have a lot of rules and where the people are happy. Be sure they teach you from the Bible because what you need to learn is what God says about things, not just what some preacher or teacher thinks. Ask God to help you find the right church for you; He knows just the right one.

NOTES

1. Oxford English Reference Dictionary, 2nd Edition, Revised. Judy Pearsall and Bill G. Trumble, Editors, Oxford, University Press, 2003, pg 783.
2. The American Heritage Dictionary of the English Language. William Morris, Editor. Houghton Mifflin Company, 1981, pg 1325.
3. Strong, James. Strongs Hebrew and Greek Dictionaries, Electronic Edition STEP Files, 2003 by Quickverse, a division of Findex.com Inc., H6754.
4. Ibid. H1823.
5. Ibid. G4982.
6. Ibid. G4991.
7. Ibid. H990.
8. Oxford English Reference Dictionary. Pg 674.
9. Strongs Hebrew & Greek Dictionary. H7646.
10. Ibid. H6529.
11. Ibid. H6310.
12. Ibid. H8193.
13. Ibid. H 4194.

14. Ibid. H 2416.
15. Ibid. H 3027.
16. Ibid. H3956.
17. Thayer's Greek Definitions, Parsons Technology, Inc., Electronic Edition STEP Files, 1999 by Findex.com, Inc. G3004.
18. Ibid. G1100.
19. Ibid. G2556.
20. Ibid. G2890.
21. Ibid. G1388.
22. Oxford English Reference Dictionary, pg 624.
23. Thayers Greek Definitions, G 18
24. Ibid. G4190.
25. Ibid. G692.
26. Ibid. G4487.
27. The Complete Word Study Dictionary: New Testament, edited by Spiros Zodhiates, Th.D. AMG Publishers, Chattanooga, TN, 1992, pg 1263.
28. Ibid. G3056.
29. The Complete Word Study Dictionary: New Testament, pg 1263.
30. Ibid. G1344.
31. Ibid. G2613.

CPSIA information can be obtained at www.ICGtesting.com
233600LV00001B/7/P

9 781414 116310